ENGINEERING ACADEMY

ENGINEER

IN TRAINING

ENGINEERING ACADEMY

STUDENT PASS

KINGFISHER
LONDON & NEW YORK

Distributed in the U.S. and Canada but Macmillan.
175 Fifth Ave., New York, NY 10010
Library of Congress Cataloging-in-Publication data has been applied for.

Series editor: Kath Jewitt
Design: Jeni Child
Consultant: Margaret Cooke BSc (Hons) CEng MIStructE

ISBN 978-0-7534-7469-3

Kingfisher books are available for special promotions and premiums.
For details contact: Special Markets Department, Macmillan,
175 Fifth Ave., New York, NY 10010.

For more information, please visit
www.kingfisherbooks.com

Printed in China
9 8 7 6 5 4 3 2 1
1TR/0119/WKT/UG/128MA

Picture credits
The Publisher would like to thank the following for permission to reproduce their material.
Top = t; Bottom = b; Center = c; Left = l; Right = r
7, 18l, 19l Shutterstock/Ethan KK; 14-15 bg (background) Shutterstock/I.Friedrich; 14tl, 15c Shutterstock/
AndreasG; 14tc Shutterstock/souta-samurai; 14tr, 14b Shutterstock/monofaction; 14cl, 15tr
Shutterstock/Magicvector; 14cr, 15tr Shutterstock/s9d9f8gj3hr; 14b, 15tl Shutterstock/Tooykrub; 14br
Shutterstock/10 FACE; 20l Shutterstock/TonyV3112; 20r Shutterstock/olavs; 24-25 bg Shutterstock/
NinaMalyina; 26c Shutterstock/Trong Nguyen; 26tr iStock/SlobodanMiljevic; 27tl Shutterstock/Fotos593;
27r iStock/mdesigner125; 30l Shutterstock/Jenson; 30r Shutterstock/Zapp2Photo; 32tl Shutterstock/
KasperczakBohdan; 32tr iStock/Lindsay imagery; 33tl iStock/Adrian Wojcik; 35 iStock/Isannes; 40tl
Shutterstock/zhu difeng; 40cr Shutterstock/Gabriele Maltinti; 40bl Shutterstock/Joaquin Ossorio
Castillo; 40br Shutterstock/Ilona Ignatova; 41tl Shutterstock/NASA images; 41tr Shutterstock/John
Selway; 41cl Shutterstock/Leonid Andronov; 41b Shutterstock/bluehand

ENGINEER

IN TRAINING

KINGFISHER

LONDON & NEW YORK

ENGINEERING ACADEMY

TRAINING PROGRAM

THEORY — **THEORY** pages are full of important information that you need to know.

PRACTICAL — **PRACTICAL** pages have a task to do or an engineering skill to acquire.

WHAT DO ENGINEERS DO?

Engineers don't just design engines, they find ways to make our lives better! An engineer has made just about everything in your world possible, including this book.

AN ENGINEER DESIGNED:

1 The machine that chopped the tree down.

2 The machine that turned the wood into paper.

3 The computer that was used to write and design the book.

4 The printing machine that put the words and pictures on the paper.

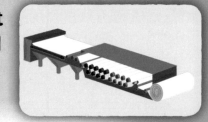

5 The ship or truck that delivered the book.

6 The building where the book was sold.

<< I design bridges strong enough to carry heavy trucks. >>

<< I design parts for electric cars that don't pollute the environment. >>

Engineers work in offices making plans and designing things on computers.

<< I think of ways to make solar panels cheaper and better. >>

<< I design robots to do jobs in factories. >>

Engineers work in laboratories testing their ideas to make sure they work.

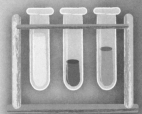

There are lots of different types of engineer. Some engineers design things that we use every day. Others design spaceships to explore Mars! Whether their inventions are big or small, engineers all use science and maths.

<< I designed this phone with a 3D camera. >>

Engineers work on the sites where things are made, to make sure their designs are built properly.

Can you find 5 differences between the two pictures?

7

THINK LIKE AN ENGINEER

So you want to be an engineer? Are you full of brilliant ideas? Do you love inventing and building things, working on a team, and solving problems? Then this is the job for you!

1. Take a problem that needs to be solved.

2. Think of different ways to solve the problem.

3. Make a plan of your best idea.

4. Build a model from your plan.

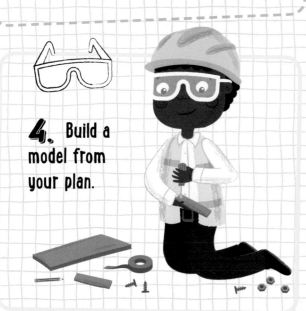

Engineers need to be good at drawing the things they want to build. Which of these hover bike designs matches the one the engineer is imagining?

a)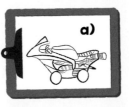

b)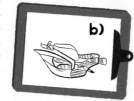

c)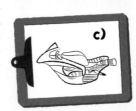

d)

5. Test out the model.

6. Think of ways to make it better.

PRACTICAL NO: 1 APPROVED

THEORY 2

CAREER FINDER

To help you work out which area of engineering is the right one for you, answer the questions and follow the trails on this career finder map.

START HERE

Then you should be...
AN ELECTRICAL ENGINEER

Then you should be...
A CHEMICAL ENGINEER

YES

NO

Would you like to work in a laboratory?

Are you fascinated by electricity?

NO

NO

YES

Are you interested in how the body works?

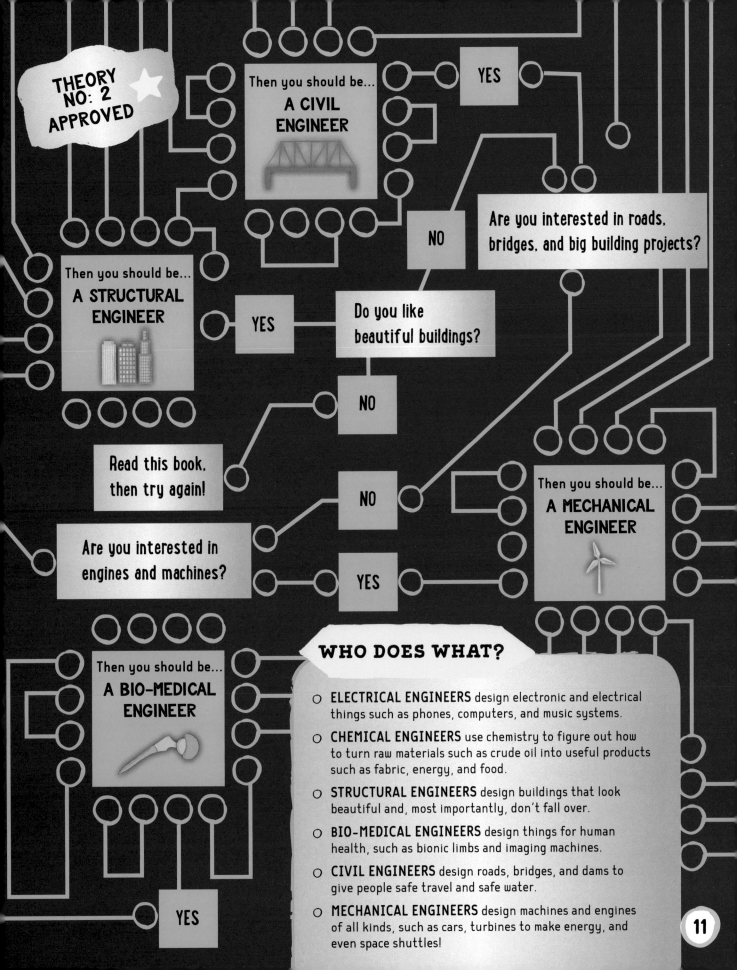

THEORY NO: 2 APPROVED ★

Then you should be...
A CIVIL ENGINEER

YES

NO

Are you interested in roads, bridges, and big building projects?

Then you should be...
A STRUCTURAL ENGINEER

YES

Do you like beautiful buildings?

NO

Read this book, then try again!

NO

Then you should be...
A MECHANICAL ENGINEER

YES

Are you interested in engines and machines?

Then you should be...
A BIO-MEDICAL ENGINEER

WHO DOES WHAT?

○ **ELECTRICAL ENGINEERS** design electronic and electrical things such as phones, computers, and music systems.

○ **CHEMICAL ENGINEERS** use chemistry to figure out how to turn raw materials such as crude oil into useful products such as fabric, energy, and food.

○ **STRUCTURAL ENGINEERS** design buildings that look beautiful and, most importantly, don't fall over.

○ **BIO-MEDICAL ENGINEERS** design things for human health, such as bionic limbs and imaging machines.

○ **CIVIL ENGINEERS** design roads, bridges, and dams to give people safe travel and safe water.

○ **MECHANICAL ENGINEERS** design machines and engines of all kinds, such as cars, turbines to make energy, and even space shuttles!

YES

ENGINEER'S KIT

Collect some useful tools from the office before you start your training. Then head for the building site to see if you can spot some engineers in action.

CHECKLIST

Can you see these things?

- ○ **Plans** to make sure the design matches what is being built.

- ○ **Tablet** to look at designs, send emails, and take pictures.

- ○ **Cell phone** to call engineers on the other side of the site.

- ○ **Safety glasses** to protect your eyes.

- ○ **Hard hat** to protect your head.

- ○ **Ear defenders** to protect your ears.

- ○ **High-vis jacket** to help you be seen.

ACTIVITY

There are lots of other people doing different jobs on the site. Can you find the below?

- ○ Builder
- ○ Carpenter
- ○ Electrician
- ○ Bricklayer

Can you also find the engineers?

Small remote-control aircraft called drones are used to fly over the site and take pictures. Can you find one?

The engineers consult the plans at every stage to make sure everything is being done correctly.

PRACTICAL NO: 2 APPROVED

GLASS

Cost	6
Strength	3
Weight	6
Recyclable	10
Waterproof	10
Flexible	0
Transparent	10
Can be shaped	9

Made from: melted sand

Used for: windows, spectacles, greenhouses, bottles, lightbulbs, drinking glasses

CONCRETE

Cost	10
Strength	7
Weight	8
Recyclable	3
Waterproof	7.5
Flexible	0
Transparent	0
Can be shaped	7

Made from: sand, gravel, cement, and water

Used for: buildings, bridges, sidewalks, roads, patios

WOOD

Cost	4
Strength	8
Weight	6
Recyclable	9
Waterproof	7.5
Flexible	10
Transparent	0
Can be shaped	5

Comes from: trees

Used for: furniture, toys, houses, doors, window frames, kitchen utensils, paper, pencils

PRACTICAL 3

MATERIALS

Everything around you is made from a material. Wood, metal, paper, or plastic—they are all materials. As an engineer, you will have to choose exactly the right material for each job.

PRACTICAL NO: 3 APPROVED

Materials can be stiff or flexible, light or heavy, hard or soft, and lots of other things too. Check out the cards above to see how each material scores. Zero is the lowest and 10 is the highest.

Here's what the symbols mean:

0	Cost
	Strength
	Weight
	Recyclable
	Waterproof
	Flexible
	Transparent (see-through)
	Can be shaped

METAL

Icon	Score
💵	8
💪	9.5
🏋	3–9
♻	8
	9
🍴	1–10
👓	0
🦕	5

Comes from: deep under the ground

Used for: bridges and buildings, cans, radiators, keys, tools

PLASTIC

Icon	Score
💵	5
💪	6
🏋	10
♻	4
💧	10
🍴	0–10
👓	0–10
	10

Made from: coal, wood, or oil

Used for: bottles, food containers, toys, bags, furniture

STONE

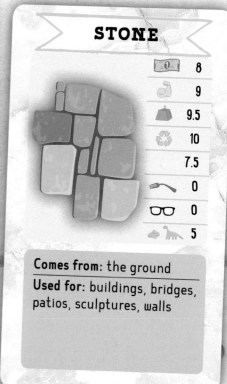

Icon	Score
💵	8
💪	9
🏋	9.5
♻	10
	7.5
🍴	0
👓	0
🦕	5

Comes from: the ground

Used for: buildings, bridges, patios, sculptures, walls

MATERIALS CHALLENGE

Look at the projects below, then check the scores on the cards above to find the best material to use for each project. The higher the score, the more suitable the material is. The material with the highest total score wins!

PROJECT 1:

Project: Design a climbing frame

Material needs to be:
- ○ Flexible
- ○ Strong
- ○ No splinters

The best material is:
- ○ Metal
- ○ Wood
- ○ Plastic

PROJECT 2:

Project: Design an aquarium

Material needs to be:
- ○ Transparent
- ○ Waterproof

The best material is:
- ○ Glass
- ○ Wood
- ○ Stone

PROJECT 3:

Project: Design an airplane

Material needs to be:
- ○ Strong
- ○ Light
- ○ Flexible

The best material is:
- ○ Concrete
- ○ Metal
- ○ Glass

BRILLIANT BRIDGES

Imagine life without bridges! You would have to cross rivers by boat, and climb up and down hills to cross valleys. Luckily, engineers design all sorts of bridges, so people can travel to where they want to go quickly and safely.

CHECKLIST

Can you find all the different kinds of bridge in the picture?

○ A **beam bridge** has strong posts to hold up the road that runs across it.

○ A **truss bridge** has a frame made out of triangles that makes the bridge very strong.

○ An **arch bridge** can have either one big arch or many smaller arches.

○ A **cable-stayed bridge** has strong cables to hold up the road. The cables are attached to tall towers.

○ A **suspension bridge** has strong cables that stretch from one side to the other. The road hangs from the cables.

ACTIVITY

1   2

3

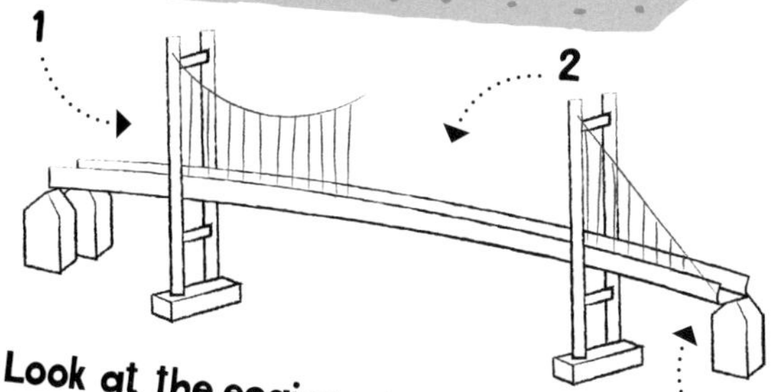

Look at the engineer's plans above. Match each part below to the plans to finish the bridge. Which part is not needed?

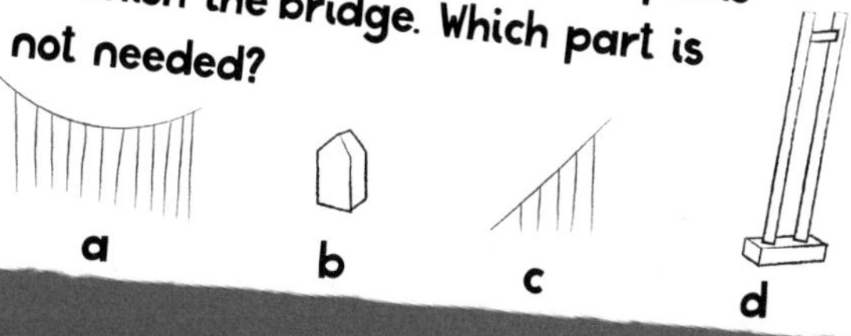

a   b   c   d

PROBLEM SOLVED!

Problem: How do tall ships pass under low bridges?
Answer: Invent bridges that can lift, tip, or open like a drawbridge.

Gateshead Millennium Bridge, England

Pont Jacques Chaban-Delmas, France

Tower Bridge, England

ON THE MOVE

Ever since the gas engine was invented, engineers have been dreaming up new ways to get from one place to another. Travel back through time to discover the story of cars.

1876

>> The first gas engine is invented.

1885

>> The first automobile goes on sale in Germany.

1908

>> A car called the Ford Model T goes on sale.

1920

>> Sports cars are built for speed. They have powerful engines and long, pointed shapes.

1930

SMOOTH SHAPES

Engineers realized that a sleek, curved shape could slip through the air smoothly, making the car go faster.

DIESEL POWER

Diesel engines run on oil. They were introduced in 1936, but became popular in the 1950s and 60s, especially for public transportation.

FIRST CARS

The first cars looked like horse carts with an engine attached. They were hard to drive and moved very slowly. Not many people could afford to buy them.

CHEAP CARS

The Model T was the first car that was affordable for ordinary people to buy. More than 15 million Model T's were produced.

>> Cars are designed to do special jobs. Police cars, ambulances, taxis, and vans are made.

SMALL CARS

More people own cars and the streets become jammed with traffic. Small cars are easy to drive in busy cities and don't use much gas.

CLEAN CARS

Electric cars are powered by electricity. They are much quieter and cleaner than gas cars. They don't create fumes that are harmful to people's health and the environment.

CARS TODAY

Engineers are now designing driverless cars that are able to drive without a human steering them. What do you think the cars of the future will be like? Do some designs and choose your best idea.

1950

>> In North America, big cars are designed that look like rockets with pointed tail fins and shiny metal.

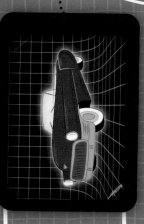

1959

>> A small car called the Mini goes on sale and is a big success.

1977

>> The first modern electric cars go on sale.

2007

>> An electric sports car is invented that runs on rechargeable batteries. It can go as fast as a gas-powered car.

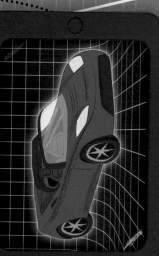
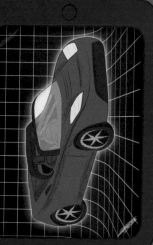

As cities grow, there is less room to build, so engineers need to find ways to fit lots of buildings into a small space. It's time to get the lowdown on building up!

THEORY 4

TALL TOWERS

STRONG AND STURDY

Skyscrapers have a stiff metal frame on the outside that is light, but strong. Thick concrete walls in the middle of the building act like a backbone to keep the skyscraper standing tall and strong.

SHARP SHAPES

Stand on one leg and you wobble, but stand with both legs wide apart and you are steady. This is why engineers design some tall towers like a triangle—wider at the bottom and narrower at the top.

DIG IT!

Before a building starts to go up, builders have to dig down. A solid base, called a foundation, is made under the ground. Thick concrete is poured in. When it sets, the concrete works like an anchor, pinning the building to the ground. It also stops the heavy building from sinking.

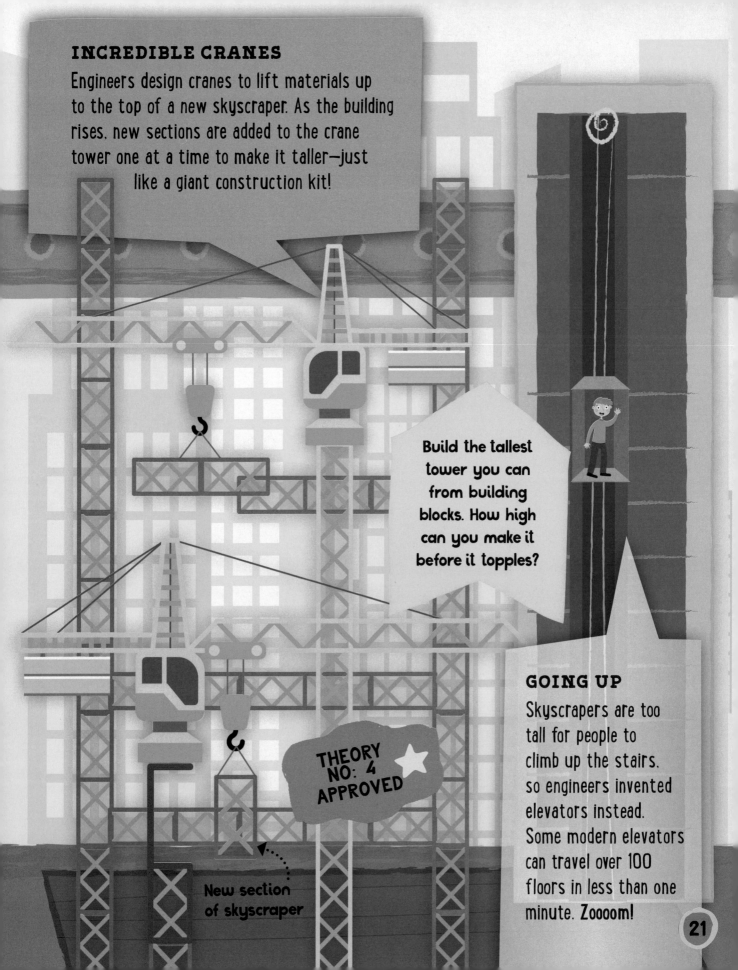

INCREDIBLE CRANES

Engineers design cranes to lift materials up to the top of a new skyscraper. As the building rises, new sections are added to the crane tower one at a time to make it taller—just like a giant construction kit!

Build the tallest tower you can from building blocks. How high can you make it before it topples?

THEORY NO: 4 APPROVED

New section of skyscraper

GOING UP

Skyscrapers are too tall for people to climb up the stairs, so engineers invented elevators instead. Some modern elevators can travel over 100 floors in less than one minute. Zoooom!

BENEATH YOUR FEET

Lots of important engineering work happens right under your feet, so put on your hard hat and head underground. There are tricky problems to be solved, and it's an engineer's job to come up with the answers.

CITY SOLUTIONS

Problem: People can't travel easily in a big city full of traffic jams.
Answer: Design a railway to carry people beneath the busy streets.

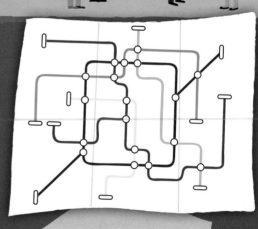

1 Escalators take people between the street and the underground railway.

2 Railway tracks, called lines, lead to places all over the city.

3 Trains travel through tunnels without getting stuck in traffic.

Can you think of names for the lines on this underground railway map?

ROAD BLOCKS

Problem: A steep mountain is stopping people from traveling to the other side.

Answer: Build a road tunnel so cars and trucks can drive through safely.

TIME TO TUNNEL

Building a tunnel is a slow, difficult job. Engineers have to plan carefully to make sure the tunnel doesn't collapse or leak if it is underwater. A giant tunneling machine breaks through underground rock with a turning wheel that cuts. These incredible machines are tunnel-boring machines, or TBMs.

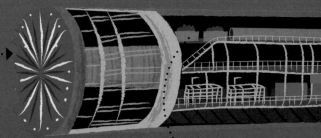

Cars to remove the rubble.

Dig a tunnel in a sandpit, big enough for a toy car to fit through. What can you find to strengthen the tunnel so it doesn't collapse? Try toilet paper rolls or small stones.

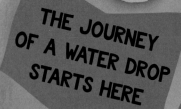

THE JOURNEY OF A WATER DROP STARTS HERE

WATER AND WASTE

Engineers design ways to clean, store, and pump water so people can have clean drinking water at the turn of a tap. Follow a drop of water on its incredible journey from the bathroom all the way back to your home.

1 Waste water runs down the drain. It leaves your home in a sewer pipe.

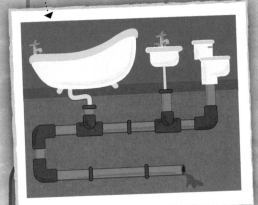

Filter beds clean the water.

2 The pipe leads to the sewage plant. Here, the water goes through many processes to remove waste and clean it.

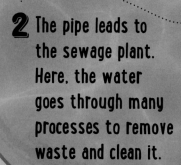

3 When the water is clean enough, it is pumped along pipes back into a river.

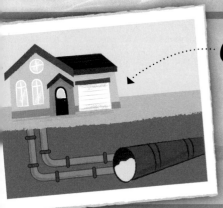

6 The treated water is clean enough to drink. It is stored in covered reservoirs, then pumped along pipes back to your home.

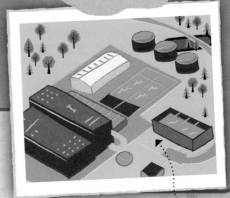

ENGINEER CHALLENGE

It's an engineer's job to find ways to save water. How many can you think of? Here's one idea to get you started:

• Turn off the water while you brush your teeth.

5 The water is then pumped to the treatment plant to be cleaned once again.

⬛ MAKING A DIFFERENCE
People dumped trash in the river below, but engineers have cleaned it up with their new water cleaning system. What has changed for the better?

4 River and rainwater are collected in a special storage lake called a reservoir.

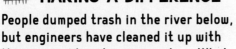

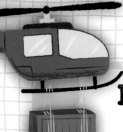

PROTECTING PEOPLE

It's time to take on wild weather and shaking quakes! Engineers have to use all their skills to help protect people before disaster strikes.

FLOODS

Floods can be caused by storms, heavy rain, or melting snow. Rivers swell and burst their banks, and water rushes down streets and floods homes and schools.

HURRICANES

Hurricanes are huge swirling storms. They bring heavy rain and super-strong winds that can rip up trees and flatten houses.

ENGINEER JOB SHEET 2:

How can engineers help? Answer: Design new and better ways to control and redirect floodwater.

ENGINEER JOB SHEET 1:

How can engineers help? Answer: Figure out ways to construct safer buildings that can stand up to powerful storms.

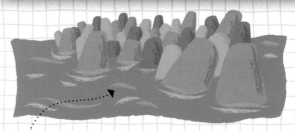

○ PLAN AHEAD

Thick walls and heavy boulders along the coast protect the land and buildings from being worn away by crashing waves.

○ TEST IT

This hurricane machine has huge fans that whip up strong winds. With its help, engineers can design windproof buildings.

BE PREPARED

These flood barriers can be slotted together quickly and easily to stop water in its tracks.

EARTHQUAKES

Earthquakes are sudden and strong movements in the ground. When pieces of Earth's surface shift, the ground shakes and buildings can collapse.

ENGINEER JOB SHEET 3:

How can engineers help? Answer: Invent equipment to test buildings and find out how strong they are.

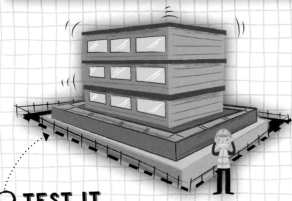

○ TEST IT

Shake tables are special platforms that are made to rock and shake, just like an earthquake. Engineers test models of quakeproof buildings to see how strong they are.

BE PREPARED

Emergency shelters are designed for people whose homes have been destroyed. These mini houses are made from strong, light materials that can be delivered easily and put up quickly.

THEORY NO: 5 APPROVED ★

Using modeling clay, build a mini flood barrier around a box in a plastic bowl. Pour in some water. Does it leak?

TORNADOES

Tornadoes are spinning columns of air that stretch from a storm cloud down to the ground. They are powerful enough to hurl cars through the air.

ENGINEER JOB SHEET 4:

How can engineers help? Answer: Experiment with shapes to find out how to reduce the effect of wind.

○ PLAN AHEAD

Square-shaped buildings have flat sides that the wind can slam into, so engineers have designed dome-shaped houses that the wind can flow over.

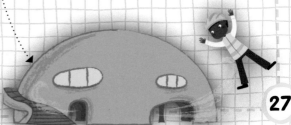

POWER UP

Flick a switch and the light comes on—easy! But where does electricity come from and how is it made? Power up your laptop for the next part of your training in renewable energy.

FOSSIL FUELS:

We burn fossil fuels such as coal, oil, and gas to produce heat energy and create electricity. This pollutes the environment, and the fossil fuels will eventually run out.

RENEWABLE ENERGY:

Engineers can develop ways to use the power of the Sun, wind, and moving water to create energy. It can even be made from the gases given off by rotting trash. These kinds of energy are much cleaner, and they will not run out. They are called renewable energy.

!
Stay safe!
· Electricity is very dangerous.
· Never play near electricity cables.
· Stay away from places marked with warning signs.

Cables carrying electricity are held above the ground by tall pylons.

🍃 TURNING TURBINES

A turbine is a wheel with blades that changes energy from waves, fuel, and wind into electricity. Wind, steam, or moving water spin the wheel really fast. This turns the generator, the machine that makes electricity.

CHECKLIST

Here are some of the ways that electricity is made. Can you spot them all in the picture?

○ **Wind turbine** This is a tall tower with huge blades at the top. Wind spins the blades to produce electricity.

○ **Solar panel** Energy from the Sun is called solar energy. Solar panels turn sunlight into electricity.

○ **Hydroelectric dam** River water is held back behind a giant dam. The water falls through pipes to turn the turbine and produce electricity.

○ **Power station** Burning coal heats water, producing steam to help make electricity. The water cools in big towers.

○ **Tidal turbine** As the tide comes in and out, it drives the blades of the turbine to produce electricity.

Which one is not a renewable source of energy?

PRACTICAL NO: 7 APPROVED

REAL-LIFE ROBOTS

Engineers design robots to do all sorts of jobs—not just the walking, talking kind of robot, but machines that follow computer instructions to do a job.

ARM ARMY

Robots are used in factories because they are really good at doing the same thing over and over again. They never get bored or tired, and they are less likely to make mistakes.

○ This car factory uses robot arms to build cars.

○ At this fruit farm, robot arms gently pick the ripest strawberries.

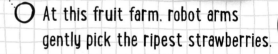

Elbow

Wrist

Shoulder

Tool

○ Robot arms swivel in all directions. The tool at the end can be changed to do different jobs.

Waist

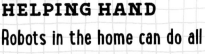
Floor-cleaning robot ⟳

ENGINEER CHALLENGE

Engineers are developing tiny robots called microbots to treat illnesses inside our bodies. Think of a job that needs doing, then draw a robot that could carry out the job.

⟳ Microbots

HELPING HAND

Robots in the home can do all sorts of jobs, such as wash and polish the floor. Some can even mow the lawn.

EXTREME ROBOTS

Engineers design robots to do jobs that are too difficult for humans. Humans could not survive on the planet Mars, but robots can. Curiosity is a roving space robot that takes pictures and sends back lots of information so we can understand more about the planet.

⟳ This small dog-like robot carries supplies into dangerous situations, such as delivering medicines into a war zone.

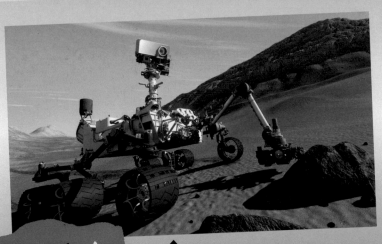

THEORY NO: 6 APPROVED

⟳ Curiosity rover

IDEAS FROM NATURE

Nature can give engineers brilliant ideas to solve some of life's problems. Take a walk on the wild side for the next part of your training.

The kingfisher's sleek beak and smooth, streamlined shape mean that it hardly makes a splash when it dives into water to catch fish.

FROM A DIVING BIRD TO ...

A shark's skin is covered with tiny scales called denticles. These help it to move swiftly through the water. The flexible scales also stop barnacles from growing on the shark.

FROM SCALY SKIN TO ...

Follow the tangled lines to discover how nature has inspired engineers.

... A WATER CATCHER

This beetle inspired inventors and engineers to find different ways to collect water from the air, such as fog catchers. These provide people who live in dry places with water to grow crops and for drinking.

... A SUPER-FAST TRAIN

The speedy Japanese Shinkansen bullet train made a loud boom as it zoomed out of tunnels—its blunt nose was to blame. Engineers fixed the problem by designing a new nose based on the kingfisher's beak.

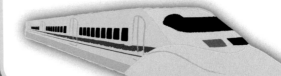

These giant muddy towers are made by termites. They keep their multistory homes cool in the hot desert by building tunnels and air holes to let stuffy air escape.

FROM MUDDY MOUNDS TO . . .

The Namibian desert beetle lives in one of the hottest, driest places on Earth. It manages to drink by catching water-filled foggy air on its bumpy back. The water trickles down to its mouth. Slurp!

FROM A BUMPY BEETLE TO . . .

. . . CLEANER, BETTER BOATS

Seaweed and barnacles grow on the bottom and sides of boats, and can slow them down. Engineers designed a special coating similar to shark skin that keeps boats clean and helps them to slip through the water.

. . . A COOL BUILDING

A team of engineers copied the clever design of a termite mound to build a shopping center in scorching Africa. It stays cool without any air conditioning.

 ENGINEER CHALLENGE
Look at the natural world around you for ideas to inspire you. What could you invent?

33

PASSENGER PLANE

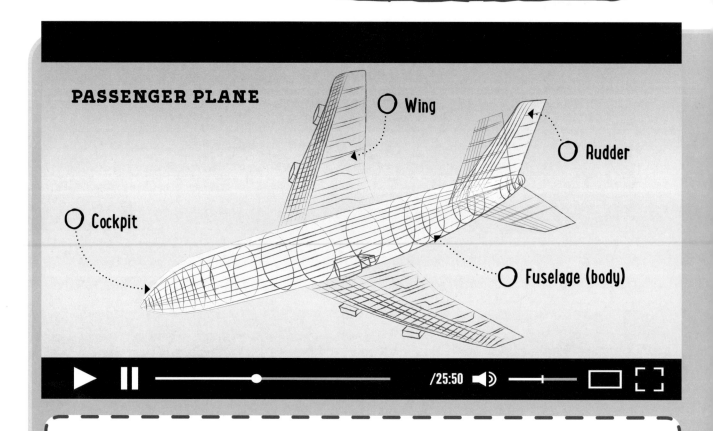

Wing

Rudder

Cockpit

Fuselage (body)

▶ ❚❚ ————————●————————— /25:50 🔊 ——|———— ▭ ⌜⌝

How does an airplane full of baggage, people, and fuel lift off the ground?

IF YOU WANT ANSWERS, THEN ASK GINA, THE AERONAUTICAL ENGINEER!

○ HOW DO YOU DESIGN AN AIRPLANE?

A team of thousands of engineers and designers spend years working on the designs for just one passenger plane. We use computer programs to help us. Everything has to be planned, from the passengers' seats to the pilots' controls. It takes about 15 years!

Design your own paper plane. Experiment with different wing shapes.

2:13

3:38

5:01

6:49

○ WHAT ARE PLANES MADE FROM?

Many planes are made from a lightweight metal called aluminum. New planes are made from a material called carbon fiber, which is stronger, stiffer, and lighter than steel.

○ HOW DOES AN AIRPLANE FLY?

It's all to do with the shape of the wing. The wing is flat on the bottom and curved on the top. The way the air flows over the top of the wing lifts the plane up.

○ WHAT MAKES THE PLANE MOVE?

The plane's jet engine gives it the power to push it forward. Blow up a balloon and then let it go. The balloon shoots forward as the air rushes out. A plane's jet engine works in a similar way.

○ HOW DO YOU KNOW THE PLANE IS SAFE?

An airplane is put through hundreds of tests before it leaves the ground. First, plane models are tested in wind tunnels and special lightning laboratories. The wings are bent to make sure they are strong, then water and ice are thrown at the engines to make sure the plane can fly, whatever the weather.

○ HOW HEAVY IS AN AIRPLANE?

A passenger plane weighs about 88,000 pounds (40,000 kilograms), but if you add the fuel, passengers, and baggage it could weigh 176,000 pounds (80,000 kilograms) when it takes off. That's as much as six double-decker buses! The plane is made of about two million parts.

PRACTICAL NO: 8 APPROVED

BODY BUILDING

Special legs made from strong, springy carbon fiber allow people with parts of their leg or foot missing to run really fast.

PROBLEM SOLVED!

Problem: Being inside a body scanning machine for a long time can be frightening.
Answer: Design scanners with headphones for listening to music, and a microphone and screen so patients can see and speak to the operator.

THEORY 8

BODY WORK

Some engineers solve problems for the human body. From designing robots that can operate on patients to building new body parts, their work helps improve and save lives!

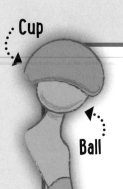

Cup

Ball

HIP REPLACEMENT

Some people need to have a hip replaced if their joint is damaged or worn out. Engineers design artificial hips made out of plastic, metal, or ceramic that can swivel just like the real joint.

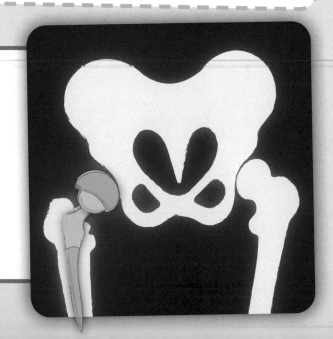

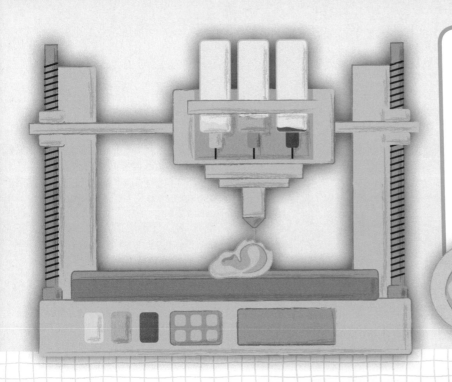

3D PRINTERS

Engineers have designed 3D printers to build solid objects, layer by layer. Melted plastic, rubber, or metal is squeezed through a nozzle, just like toothpaste. The printers can be used to make anything, including replacement noses and ears!

ACTIVITY

Which one of these items cannot be made using a 3D printer?

Tooth

Ear

Bone

Brain

BODY DETECTIVES

Engineers have even created machines to work inside the body. This pill-shaped camera is small enough for the patient to swallow! It travels through the body, taking pictures of the intestines along the way.

Actual size

1 INCH
(2.5 CM)

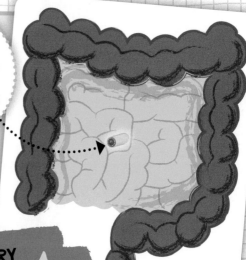

THEORY
NO: 6
APPROVED

37

EXPLORING THE OCEANS

To complete your training, let's plunge into the deep ocean—the most unexplored place on Earth. It's cold, dark, and dangerous, but marine engineers have designed vehicles that make it possible to explore its depths.

ROV (REMOTELY OPERATED VEHICLE)

These underwater robots are used when water is too deep or dangerous for divers.

Thick cable attached to the boat allows operators on board to control the ROV

Robotic arms do difficult jobs

SUBMARINE

Its double walls are made from strong metal. The gap between the walls fills with air or water to make the submarine rise or sink.

Periscope to see above water

Propeller to move through the water

FEEL THE PRESSURE!

It's difficult to explore the deep ocean because the weight of all the water above is so heavy that it would crush most things. This is called water pressure. The deeper you go, the higher the pressure becomes.

656 FEET (200 METERS) DEEP
SUNLIT ZONE

3280 FEET (1000 METERS) DEEP
TWILIGHT ZONE

SUBMERSIBLE

These small submarines carry just a few crew members. They have bright lights to see in the dark water.

Robotic arm to collect things

ENGINEER CHALLENGE

Put your hand inside a plastic bag, then plunge your hand into a bucket of water. Can you feel the bag pressing against your skin? This is the weight of the water, or the water pressure, pushing on your hand.

13,123 FEET (4000 METERS) DEEP
MIDNIGHT ZONE

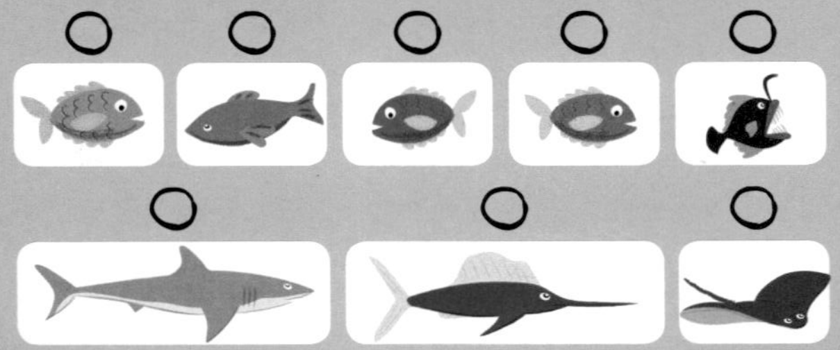

DEEP DOWN

Deepsea Challenger explored the deepest place on Earth—the Mariana Trench in the Pacific Ocean, which is about 6 miles (11 kilometers) deep.

THEORY
NO: 9
APPROVED

ACTIVITY

Can you find all these fish in the picture?

19,685 FEET (6000 METERS) DEEP
ZERO SUNLIGHT ZONE

39

AMAZING ENGINEERING

If there's a problem, engineers will find a way to solve it. Take this tour to check out some incredible feats of engineering!

○ MEGA DOME

The Pantheon in Rome is an ancient domed temple built 2,000 years ago. It is made from a material similar to modern-day concrete, which is why it has lasted so well.

○ WONDER WALL

The Great Wall of China is one of the largest artificial structures ever built. It stretches for 13,000 miles (21,000 kilometers), and was designed to keep out invaders.

○ SUPER TOWER

The Burj Khalifa is a record-breaking 160-story skyscraper in the city of Dubai. It is 2,700 feet (828 meters) high, and the concrete used to build the tower weighs as much as 100,000 elephants.

○ HIGH ROAD

At 1,125 feet (343 meters) high, the Millau Viaduct, in France, is the tallest bridge in the world. It was built to stop traffic jams in the valley below during the busy summer vacation.

○ SUPERSONIC

Concorde was the fastest airliner ever. It could reach 1,353 miles (2,179 kilometers) per hour and was faster than the speed of sound. Its long, pointed arrow shape helped it to slip smoothly through the air.

○ SPACE CITY

The International Space Station is the largest spacecraft ever built. It is so huge that it was built on Earth and taken into space piece by piece. Sixteen giant solar panels turn the Sun's energy into electricity for the Space Station.

○ CLEVER COMPUTERS

The first computers, made in the 1940s, were as big as a large room. Today, computers are much smaller and are used everywhere. They control lots of useful things, from washing machines to driverless trains. Virtual reality (VR) computers use sights and sounds to make us believe we are in a totally different place.

○ CELL MANIA

Cell phones are used all over our planet. The first ones were as big as a brick, but now tiny electronic parts make them small enough to fit in your pocket. Smartphones are like mini computers—they can be used for gaming, searching the internet, and watching movies.

Can you name another example of amazing engineering?

ISAMBARD KINGDOM BRUNEL

Brunel designed bridges, tunnels, railways, and steamships using new materials and methods. His work helped people travel more easily.

THE WRIGHT BROTHERS

Wilbur and Orville Wright designed, built and flew the first successful airplane. The first flight lasted only 12 seconds, but it was the beginning of air travel.

EMILY ROEBLING

Emily Roebling took over her husband's job as chief engineer when he became ill and oversaw the building of the Brooklyn Bridge in New York.

THOMAS EDISON

Edison came up with inventions to make life better. He created the first working lightbulb and the kinetoscope, a machine for viewing moving pictures.

HALL OF FAME

JOHN LOGIE BAIRD

Baird built the first television from odds and ends, including a cookie tin and a hat box. The image on the screen was fuzzy, but it showed moving pictures!

STEPHANIE KWOLEK

This chemical engineer saves lives with her super-strong material called Kevlar. It is used to make bulletproof vests and helmets, and even spacesuits.

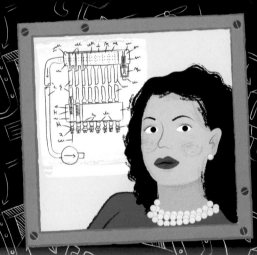

HEDY LAMARR

This famous Hollywood star was also a top engineer. During the Second World War she invented a secret communication system.

DR. WANDA AUSTIN

Dr. Wanda Austin is an award-winning aeronautical engineer, who is internationally recognized for her work on the US Space Program.

These engineers have all helped make things possible with their amazing work. Will you be the next engineer to create something incredible?

EXAMINATION

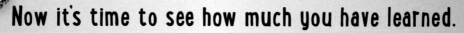

Now it's time to see how much you have learned.

1 How long did it take to build the Great Wall of China?
- a) 5 years
- b) 200 years
- c) Over 1,000 years

2 How many floors can a modern elevator travel up and down?
- a) 9
- b) 50
- c) over 100

3 What is concrete used for?
- a) Faucets, radiators, and washing machines
- b) Windows, lightbulbs, and greenhouses
- c) Buildings, sidewalks and bridges

4 Which of these materials is waterproof?
- a) Wood
- b) Plastic
- c) Paper

5 Which of these is a type of bridge?
- a) Suspension bridge
- b) Pension bridge
- c) Dimension bridge

6 Which shape do engineers use to build strong bridges and buildings?
- a) Star
- b) Oval
- c) Triangle

7 Which was the first model of car cheap enough for ordinary people to buy?
- a) Model P Ford
- b) Model C Ford
- c) Model T Ford

8 What kind of shape makes vehicles slip through the air quickly?
- a) Smooth and sleek
- b) Big and round
- c) Wavy and wide

9 Which type of car is best for the environment?

a) Gas

b) Diesel

c) Electric

10 What is the underground base of a building called?

a) The foundation

b) The operation

c) The hesitation

11 What is another name for a giant tunnelling machine?

a) Funnel Boring Machine

b) Tunnel Boring Machine

c) Tunnel Coring Machine

12 What do sewer pipes carry?

a) Fresh water

b) Waste water

c) Music

13 What is a shake table?

a) Machine to test tables

b) Machine to test quakeproof buildings

c) Table with a wobbly leg

14 Which of these IS a source of renewable energy?

a) Wind

b) Coal

c) Crude oil

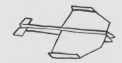

ENGINEERING SCORES

Check your answers at the back of the book and add up your score.

1 to 5 Oops! Go back to Engineering Academy and study your facts.

6 to 10 You are well on your way to becoming a super engineer.

11 to 14 Top of the class! You could be the next great engineer!

ENGINEER SPEAK

aluminum
A very lightweight metal, often used to build aircraft.

body scanning machine
An electronic machine that produces detailed pictures of the inside of the body.

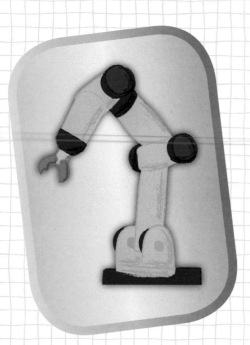

cement
Something used in building to hold bricks together.

concrete
A mixture of cement and sand used for making buildings, paths, and bridges.

diesel engine
A kind of engine that uses oil as fuel.

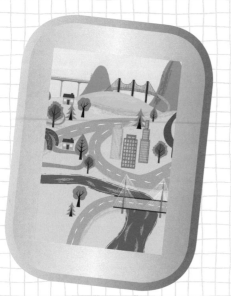

drone
A small aircraft that is controlled by someone on the ground.

engineer's plans
An engineer's drawings with measurements, to show how to build something.

fossil fuel
Fuels, such as coal and oil, that are formed underground from plant and animal remains.

laboratory
A room or building that is equipped for experiments and research.

microbots

Tiny robots designed to perform a particular task or job. They can be less than 1/25 inch (one millimeter) in size.

ore

Any rock or soil that contains metal.

streamlined

Designed and built in a way that makes movement through air or water easier.

transparent

A material so clear that you can see through it.

turbine

A type of machine with blades and a special wheel that turns to make power.

ENGINEERING ACADEMY

WELL DONE!

You made it through your engineer training.

Name...

FULLY QUALIFIED

ENGINEER

ANSWERS

Page 7
The five differences are circled below:

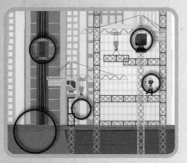

Page 9
The bike that matches is C.

Pages 12-13
The things to find are circled below:
Occupations = Green circles
Checklist = Pink circles

The engineers are all wearing red.

The drone is circled blue.

Page 15
Project 1 = plastic
Project 2 = glass
Project 3 = metal

Pages 16-17
The things to find are circled below:

The part that isn't needed is: d

Page 25
The river now has clean water,
no trash in it, more wildlife,
and no flies.

Page 29
The things to find are circled below:

The power station is not a renewable
source of energy.

Page 32-33
Kingfisher = super-fast bullet train

Shark skin = shark-skin coating on
boats to keep them clean and streamlined.

Termite towers = African
shopping center

Namibian desert beetle = water
collection system

Page 37
Brain

Page 39
The things to find are circled below:

Page 44
1 = c; 2 = c; 3 = c; 4 = b; 5 = a;
6 = c, 7 = c, 8 = a; 9 = c; 10 = a;
11 = b; 12 = b; 13 = b; 14 = a